Roadrunners

By JoAnn Early Macken

Reading Consultant: Jeanne Clidas, Ph.D.
Director, Roberts Wesleyan College Literacy Clinic

WEEKLY READER®
PUBLISHING

Please visit our web site at **www.garethstevens.com.**
For a free catalog describing our list of high-quality books,
call 1-877-542-2595 (USA) or 1-800-387-3178 (Canada).
Our fax: 1-877-542-2596

Library of Congress Cataloging-in-Publication Data

Macken, JoAnn Early, 1953–
      Roadrunners / by JoAnn Early Macken; reading consultant, Jeanne Clidas.
         p. cm. — (Animals that live in the desert)
      Includes bibliographical references and index.
      ISBN-10: 1-4339-2391-2   ISBN-13: 978-1-4339-2391-3 (lib. bdg.)
      ISBN-10: 1-4339-2452-8   ISBN-13: 978-1-4339-2452-1 (soft cover)
      1. Roadrunner—Juvenile literature. I. Title.
    QL696.C83M333   2010
    598.7'4—dc22
                                     2009002865

This edition first published in 2010 by
Weekly Reader® Books
An Imprint of Gareth Stevens Publishing
1 Reader's Digest Road
Pleasantville, NY 10570-7000 USA

Executive Managing Editor: Lisa M. Herrington
Senior Editor: Barbara Bakowski
Project Management: Spooky Cheetah Press
Cover Designers: Jennifer Ryder-Talbot and Studio Montage
Production: Studio Montage
Library Consultant: Carl Harvey, Library Media Specialist, Noblesville, Indiana

Photo credits: Cover, pp. 1, 7 Shutterstock; p. 5 © David Kjaer/naturepl.com; p. 9 © Marilyn Moseley LaMantia/
Graphicstock 2005; p. 11 © David Welling/naturepl.com; p. 13 © John Cancalosi/naturepl.com; p. 15 © Arthur
Morris/Visuals Unlimited; p. 17 © Jeff Foott/naturepl.com; p. 19 © Rolf Nussbaumer; p. 21 © Tom and Pat Leeson

Printed in the United States of America

1 2 3 4 5 6 7 8 9 14 13 12 11 10 09

Table of Contents

Desert Birds 4

Built for Speed 10

Raising a Family 16

Glossary 22

For More Information 23

Index 24

Boldface words appear in the glossary.

Desert Birds

Roadrunners are black, brown, and white birds. They can fly, but they usually stay on the ground. Most of the time, they walk or run across the **desert**.

Roadrunners have long tails and short wings. When they run, their tails and wings help them balance.

tail

wing

A roadrunner has a **crest** on its head. The crest is made of feathers. The bird has a long, strong **beak**.

crest

beak

9

Built for Speed

Roadrunners have long legs. On each foot, two toes point forward. Two toes point back.

toes

Roadrunners run fast!
They chase **prey**, such as
insects, lizards, and mice.
Roadrunners even eat
rattlesnakes!

prey (lizard)

When the desert is hot, roadrunners rest in the shade. When it is cold, they **roost** in trees. They warm up in the sun.

Raising a Family

Roadrunners build nests out of sticks. They lay eggs in the nests. The parents keep the eggs warm until the babies **hatch**.

The baby birds are called **chicks**. The parents feed them and keep them safe.

chicks

The chicks learn to fly. They stay near the nest for a week or two. Then they go off into the desert.

Fast Facts

Height	about 21 inches (53 centimeters)
Wingspan	about 19 inches (48 centimeters)
Weight	about 19 ounces (454 grams)
Diet	insects, lizards, and snakes
Average life span	up to 8 years

Glossary

beak: the bill of a bird

chicks: baby birds

crest: a bunch of long feathers on the head of a bird

desert: a dry area with little rainfall

hatch: to come out of an egg

prey: animals that are killed for food

roost: to rest or settle down on a perch

For More Information

Books

Roadrunners. My Big Backyard (series). Lola M. Schaefer (Heinemann, 2004)

Roadrunners. Look West (series). Lynn Hassler Kaufman. (Rio Nuevo Publishers, 2005)

Web Sites

Greater Roadrunner

www.birds.cornell.edu/AllAboutBirds/BirdGuide/ Greater_Roadrunner.html
Hear a roadrunner's song. Learn more about this desert bird.

Greater Roadrunner

www.passporttotexas.com/birds/jul00.html
Listen to the call of a roadrunner.

Index

beaks 8

chicks 18, 20

crests 8

eating 12, 18

eggs 16

flying 4, 20

hatching 16

legs 10

nests 16, 20

roosting 14

running 4, 6, 12

tails 6

toes 10

wings 6

About the Author

JoAnn Early Macken is the author of two rhyming picture books, *Sing-Along Song* and *Cats on Judy*, and more than 80 nonfiction books for children. Her poems have appeared in several children's magazines. She lives in Wisconsin with her husband and their two sons.